GROWING COURAGE

Self-Empowerment for Facing Life's Challenges
Quotes, Stories and Insights

Alberta V. Fredricksen

HeartPeace Now

HeartPeace Now Publications

GROWING COURAGE

Alberta Fredricksen
P.O. Box 10312
Bozeman, MT 59719
Alberta@HeartPeaceNow.com
www.HeartPeaceNow.com

ISBN: 978-0-9844015-4-3
Editing by Gwen Hoffnagle

The purpose of this book is to educate, inspire and entertain. The author and publisher shall have no liability for the use of the information contained in this book.

DEDICATION

To all the courageous teachers in my life, beginning with my parents, for keeping the faith, holding higher intentions and a steady balance, and gently leading through wisdom, right confrontation and the courage to create greater understanding, stronger relationships, more and better communication and a shared responsibility for community—I am grateful!

PRAISE FOR *GROWING COURAGE*

One word resonated through my mind as I read *Growing Courage*: bracing. This short book carries a profound and empowering message – that you have the seeds of courage inside you and those seeds can grow. Read *Growing Courage* whenever you feel afraid or unable to cope with the circumstances of your life. The wisdom in these pages will call forth new courage and help you walk boldly through any circumstance.
~Lynne Klippel, bestselling author of *Overcomers, Inc.*

Thank you for such a profound and well-thought-out teaching on courage, a virtue so essential for our personal self-mastery and for the spiritual victory of this planet.
~Therese Emmanuel Grey, author of *Miracles, Masters and Mirth* and *The Four Faces of God Shine through Me.*

By the time I finished reading *Growing Courage*, I realized that I myself had experienced a growing commitment to be more courageous and true to myself. Well done!
~Nancy Showalter, author of the award-winning book *It's OK to Be Rich: The Entrepreneur's Guide to Increased Wealth and Personal Mastery.* www.itsok2berich.com

Alberta breaks down the real meaning of the word *courage*—to do what is right and is not defined by the size or scope of the act. By helping us to recognize the many ways we are already acting courageously, Alberta empowers us to even greater works.
~Rev. Linda Czaplinski

Alberta Velma Fredricksen has had to face those things that go bump in the night. This challenge that comes to all of us is often faced, overcome and put behind us as quickly as possible. There are great lessons of courage not shared because of how personal it appeared to be. Alberta, like all great teachers, wishes to share her insight into this vulnerable, adrenaline-inducing moment, when one must choose the beneficent over the reactionary. Sometimes it happens when your own blood fills your mouth and other times when it is so subtle that only you and your God know. In this little book, Alberta wholeheartedly seeks to help you know and face your day of "Courage" with personal success.

~Brian Emmanuel Grey, co-author of *Why We Do What We Do* and *The Psychology of Success*

What a wonderful little book! How precious a gift it is when someone who exemplifies a virtue opens the door to the quotes, stories and experiences that motivated them on their journey to mastery. Alberta presents this material in a well-planned, cohesive fashion, pacing our growth in understanding to the very end. I thoroughly enjoyed and was inspired by this book as I'm sure anyone interested in the perfection of virtue will be.

~Karleen McSherry, author of *Letters from the Unborn*

Sometimes we need that extra hug. A friend to reach out in compassion and a big embrace with words of encouragement that connect deep within our soul to bring out the best from within us. Somehow that simple, but wise and loving act renews us to move forward when life's challenges seem a little too hard to bear alone.

In real time, that essence is what Alberta brings, whether as a friend, teacher, author, or *Transforming Conflict* and spiritual life coach. To me, that is the gem of inspiration, comfort, and encouragement you will discover in this little book to *grow* and *strengthen* the virtue of courage.

Alberta says, "The seed is already within you." As you read and contemplate this delightful resource, *Growing Courage*, I believe the roots of that "seed within you" may very well reach deep within the soil of consciousness through these many stories, perspectives, and deeper insights to help create a mighty oak—a fortress of courage. Alberta has an uncanny knack of getting through the obvious to nourish the inner life.

~Janette Mathis, co-founder, Inner Artz: *Images that Elevate*

With uncommon care, perception and logic, Alberta Fredricksen creates another inspirational book for times of strife or need into a journey you'll want to take, not just read about. I was surprised at the impact this little book made on me. Beyond information, this reading became an experience and the message sank deep.

Alberta illustrates that the path to grow courage uses the principle of good will to grow your real self, your community and our world. Have the courage to keep several copies available for gifts and share it everywhere. *Growing Courage* will make a difference and you will make a difference. And after all, isn't that what we all want?
~Antonia Johnson, Quantum Counselor, TREEwork

Thank you, Alberta, for once again drawing together such soul-provoking seeds to grow our awareness of another precious quality of the heart—courage. Spiritual teachers remind us that a pure heart can more readily become an open heart—a heart open to the deepest truths of our existence. This is more than just a collection of inspiring insights. This is an irresistible dance with courage.
~Marcia Marie Scully, founder of www.5elementfoods.com

You will want to keep this precious little book close to your heart. It will inspire you for the times you need more courage for what you must do. It will provide hope for being courageous in the future, no matter how things might have seemed in the past. Most of us need such reminders in this hour on planet Earth. Thank you, Alberta!
~Caroline Hanstke, psychologist, author of *The Science of the Conversion of the Holy Spirit in the New Jerusalem*

TABLE OF CONTENTS

CHAPTER 1:
Introduction

Courage! Courage is something most of us admire and respect in others. And perhaps we wonder if others would find this quality in us. We hope that when put to the test, we will be able to dig deep and find this virtue within us in the times and circumstances required in an emergency or when others are really counting on us.

I believe all of us have courage within us. It manifests in many ways. It's not always a heroic rescue of some other living creature or placing your physical life in jeopardy on behalf of someone or some cause. Courage has many faces and shows up in your daily life in what may seem like ordinary events and conversations.

We learn from observing all these events and conversations, even if they were not our direct experiences. When we hear the stories of others' experiences in life and read what others have said about what they learned or perceived, we can apply the wisdom gained and shared by them to our own lives.

As a teacher and a conflict and life coach, I learn from the people I am privileged to work with through what they have experienced, what they have learned, and what they say about those experiences. Conflict provides fertile ground for courage to emerge. And I have learned that many people avoid conflict because they are afraid. They fear that they will not be able to succeed or they will be made to appear wrong in the eyes of others. If they experience fear, they often believe they lack the courage to confront and deal with the conflicts in their daily lives. So they don't try or they withdraw, or they may respond with anger or frustration that comes from not knowing what else to do.

It is rewarding to participate in the peacemaking process. And it does require some courage. As we gain communication skills, learning what to say or write and what to do and when to do it, we are *growing* our courage. The most important thing to know is that the seed of courage is already within you. And you can nurture its growth as you nurture other living things.

I remember my first visit to the big island of Hawaii and walking over the cooled lava sheets and seeing a single coffee tree sprouting out of the hard, black lava. I was astounded that this bright, green shoot could come from a seed and manage to break through the hard surface. Perhaps the delivery system for the seed had been the warm trade winds, or a bird flying over. There it was—this vibrant, green, solitary shoot of a coffee tree, all alone in the large black expanse of lava. And I actually thought that this had to be a very courageous seed that was determined to become what it was intended to be in such a harsh environment. It was thrusting upward toward the bright shaft of sunlight that was nourishing the sprout and lighting the way.

I share this book of quotations on *Courage* with you with the hope and prayer that you and I can gain inspiration. And then we can nurture the acorn of courage within each of us and allow it to blossom into the mighty oak that represents everything we were intended to be in this life.

"We live in a conscious universe where everything is connected and every situation is driven by potential."
~Dr. Vernon Woolf, founder of the Academy of Holodynamics

We are empowered to draw upon that quality—that virtue—of courage within us to harmonize and build stronger relationships with individuals and in groups wherever we are planted.

May the quotes selected for *Growing Courage* be an impetus for each one to reveal the many faces of courage that can assist you in growing courage and delivering your unique gifts to a waiting world.

HeartPeace to You,
Alberta V. Fredricksen

CHAPTER 2:
Courage as a Virtue

"Courage is not simply one of the virtues, but the form of every virtue at the testing point, which means at the point of highest reality."
~C. S. Lewis, *The Screwtape Letters*

Most of us admire those who have been hailed as heroes, having performed some super-human feat because they were the ones who seemed to have more courage than others around them at that moment in time.

"You will never do anything in this world without courage. It is the greatest quality of the mind next to honor."
~Aristotle

Who are those individuals who feel empowered to act—to speak? Where did they find that courage? Was it always within them? Was it a part of their special calling in life? Is it only for a special few? Is it a part of your calling—your life?

There are many virtues that we can pursue and grow in addition to courage: kindness, patience, mercy, honor, truthfulness, charity, and on and on. The virtues are like the radiant aspects of a rainbow. And mankind has been given the freedom to choose from among the infinite virtues of Good instead of choosing from the infinite manifestations of evil.

"The more you witness virtues in action, the better you'll understand them. You need very clear understandings of virtues if you are to get them. And you need equally clear understandings of vices, and their consequences, if you are to steer clear of them."
~William J. Bennett

I believe that courage is a virtue that already exists in all of us to some extent. There are aspects of character that you might not have previously identified as courage in yourself. And each of us can choose to practice, grow and make the virtue of courage more present in our lives.

This is the very essence of character development. Even as we teach children, we can teach ourselves to take on a virtue of a teacher or someone we respect or admire—someone who has inspired us, such as Christ, Buddha, Mother Teresa, George Washington, Mahatma Gandhi or Aleksandr Solzhenitsyn. When you choose to put on the virtues you have perceived in others who have lived lives of inspiration, you develop a stronger relationship with your own higher Source and are more empowered to resist the temptations of your lower self or of negative social and cultural influences.

> *"When I was a young man, I wanted to change the world. I found it was difficult to change the world, so I tried to change my nation. When I found I couldn't change the nation, I began to focus on my town. I couldn't change the town and as an older man, I tried to change my family.*
>
> *Now, as an old man, I realize the only thing I can change is myself, and suddenly I realize that if long ago I had changed myself, I could have made an impact on my family. My family and I could have made an impact on our town. Their impact could have changed the nation and I could indeed have changed the world."*
> ~Unknown monk circa 1100 AD

Knowing what's real about yourself and what your needs are, you can make better progress toward becoming who you really are and accomplishing what you came to do.

> *"It takes courage to grow up and become who you really are."*
> ~E. E. Cummings

"Strength does not come from physical capacity. It comes from an indomitable will."
~Mahatma Gandhi

Virtue itself is a virtue. Consider which virtue you might already manifest in some ways. Perhaps others have commented about a special quality within you or a way of being in the world that you bring forth consistently. Perhaps there is a virtue that you would like to choose to grow and build a momentum on. The gift of growing a virtue is that you can be better prepared and able to empower others through that virtue. Your demonstration of that virtue becomes a presence of that virtue's qualities in life that can be seen or experienced by others, and that can serve as an example to others.

"I'd rather see a sermon than hear one any day;
I'd rather one should walk with me than merely tell the way."
~Edgar A. Guest, *Sermons We See*

As you practice and put on the virtue you pursue, it can become like a favorite garment, one that you are comfortable wearing and being present with without even noticing it.

"Virtue owns no master. He who honors her shall have more of her,
and he who slights her less. The responsibility lies with the chooser.
Heaven is guiltless."
~Plato, Book 10 of *The Republic*

CHAPTER 3:

Claim the Flame of Courage

"*Courage is the most important of all the virtues because without courage, you can't practice any other virtue consistently.*"
~Maya Angelou

Courage can be like a song within you. And sometimes it even rhymes. I wrote the poem that follows, called "Claim the Flame of Courage," at a time when I needed courage but wasn't sure I really had it. I really did not know if I could bear or have the courage to get through the circumstances before me. So I searched for inspiration and found many profound quotations from others that have *encouraged* me to take on growing the virtue of courage. These words of others helped me find my words, my ways of expressing courage.

I was *encouraged* by others. It's interesting to note how this very powerful word we have for helping and empowering others to move toward their dreams and goals—to *encourage*—has "courage" as its root. And if we *discourage* others, whether intended or not, it might be as if we have pulled out or uprooted that young, tender green shoot before it could become what it was meant to be.

So discernment is needed, and this is another aspect of character development that we should all cultivate within ourselves. For instance, in raising children there are behaviors and actions that we believe must be *discouraged* for safety or for the success of the child. Learning how to communicate about such things while *encouraging* the child's best qualities to continue to learn and grow becomes our goal.

"*Courage is contagious. When a brave man takes a stand, the spines of others are often stiffened.*"
~Billy Graham, *Reader's Digest*, July 1964

*"See…how your courage begets courage and how that which you
have become and sustained can draw to you greater and greater
reinforcement."*[1]
~Ascended Lady Master Venus

Claim the Flame of Courage

To claim the flame of courage
Takes attainment of the heart.
When like a lion roaring,
Fear and doubt must soon depart.

Courage can be watchfulness
As the defender on the wall,
Wary of every form of consciousness
That would entrap or enthrall.

Courage is endurance,
Cheerfulness, day and night.
Unified with your true Self
When you become more Light.

Courage is aligned
With steadiness, hand in hand.
When you display the constancy,
See your consciousness expand.

Courage is the mark
Of those who choose to win.
Dissolving errors of the past,
You lead others to begin.

Courage is for mastery;
The heart, it comes of age.
With heavenly friends to assist you,
You attain a brand new stage.

by Alberta Fredricksen, *Transforming Everyday Conflict*[2]

Elements of this poem give voice to other meanings of the word *courage*. We capture other descriptors like:

- Attainment
- Maturity of heart
- Watchfulness as a form of consciousness
- Endurance
- Cheerfulness
- Constancy and steadiness
- A consciousness of winning
- Leading others to begin and try

And TRY we must! How do we know that we can or cannot accomplish courageous feats of the body, the mind or the Spirit if we don't TRY? We strive to prove the formula T + R + Y, an initialism for Theos + Rule + You.[3] Saint Germain, a master alchemist, taught that this is essentially man making Spirit's laws active in our own beings and our own self-awareness. He encourages us to *try* as we learn to exercise our God-given faculties.

> *"Man cannot discover new oceans unless he has courage*
> *to lose sight of the shore."*
> ~Unknown

> *"Being vulnerable doesn't have to be threatening. Just have the*
> *courage to be sincere, open and honest. This opens the door to*
> *deeper communication all around. It creates self-empowerment and*
> *the kind of connections with others we all want in life. Speaking*
> *from the heart frees us from the secrets that burden us. These secrets*
> *are what make us sick or fearful. Speaking truth helps you get*
> *clarity on your real heart directives.*
> ~Sara Paddison, *The Hidden Power of the Heart*

CHAPTER 4:

Courage Is...

"Courage is the virtue that President Kennedy most admired. He sought out those people who had demonstrated in some way, whether it was on a battlefield or a baseball diamond, in a speech or fighting for a cause, that they had courage that they would stand up, that they could be counted on."
~Robert F. Kennedy, in the foreword to *Profiles in Courage*

President John F. Kennedy's Pulitzer-Prize-winning book published in 1957, *Profiles in Courage,*[4] is about his admiration for the courage shown by elected leaders in the face of adverse factions that pulled these individuals in different directions. He wrote:

"This is a book about that most admirable of human virtues—courage. 'Grace under pressure,' Ernest Hemingway defined it."[5]

"In whatever area in life one may meet the challenges of courage, whatever may be the sacrifices he faces if he follows his conscience—the loss of his friends, his fortune, his contentment, even the esteem of his fellow men—each man must decide for himself the course he will follow. The stories of past courage can define that ingredient—they can teach, they can offer hope, they can provide inspiration. But they cannot supply courage itself. For this each man must look into his own soul."[6]

"For without belittling the courage with which men have died, we should not forget those acts of courage with which men—such as the subjects of this book—have lived."[7]
~John F. Kennedy

"A decline in courage may be the most striking feature that an outside observer notices in the West today. The Western world has lost its civic courage...Such a decline in courage is particularly noticeable among the ruling and intellectual elite, causing an impression of a loss of courage by the entire society."
~Aleksandr Solzhenitsyn

At one point in my life, I was working as the personnel director at a state prison for men. I had taken a new position and moved alone to a new state and community, and it was a lonely outpost for me. I wondered if I had made a big mistake and feared that I might not be able to do what I had intended. I decided to wear an Archangel Michael medal around my neck to remind me of my personal need for protection and courage, and to remind me to stay spiritually connected to my higher Source.

A dictionary definition of courage is "the ability to face difficulty or danger with firmness and without fear." One day, as I was browsing in a used book store in this new community, I found a book entitled *Courage* by Jon Johnson.[8] Johnson said courage was "the ability and commitment to *endure and challenge* difficulty or danger with firmness *in spite* of fear."[9] This resonated with me.

"Courage is resistance to fear, mastery of fear—not absence of fear."
~Mark Twain

*"Bran thought about it. 'Can a man still be brave if he's afraid?'
'That is the only time a man can be brave,' his father told him."*
~George R. R. Martin, *A Game of Thrones*

In trying to understand the meaning of courage, you can find thirty-plus synonyms for the word. This illustrates how much the virtue of courage is embedded in all of our lives and can be expanded in ways you may never have thought of previously as courageous.

Author Jon Johnson expands on several different ways of perceiving and demonstrating courage.

FORTITUDE might be described as "biting the bullet" or taking punishing licks or fighting back after a devastating illness—a kind of courage associated with great athletes.[10]

> *"I've missed more than 9,000 shots in my career. I've lost almost 300 games. 26 times I've been trusted to take the game-winning shot and missed. I've failed over and over and over again in my life. And that is why I succeed."*
> ~Michael Jordan

> *"My attitude is that if you push me towards a weakness, I will turn that weakness into a strength."*
> ~Michael Jordan

BRAVERY is best understood as the kind of courage that responds to a crisis; it often occurs in real-life dramas.[11]

> *"You can't relate to a superhero, to a superman, but you can identify with a real man who in times of crisis draws forth some extraordinary quality from within himself and triumphs but only after a struggle."*
> ~Timothy Dalton

> *"Loyalty and devotion lead to bravery. Bravery leads to the spirit of self-sacrifice. The spirit of self-sacrifice creates trust in the power of love."*
> ~Morihei Ueshiba

> *"A brave man acknowledges the strength of others."*
> ~Veronica Roth, *Divergent*

VALOR is how courage is often referred to on the battlefield. Soldiers with valor tend to be infused and motivated by intense patriotism, an elevated morale and a tendency to be very optimistic about their chances for victory.[12] This is often the case when faced with overwhelming odds, like David facing Goliath or like King Leonidas and the 300 Spartans holding the pass at Thermopylae against hundreds of thousands of Persians.

"Battle is the most magnificent competition in which a human being can indulge. It brings out all that is best; it removes all that is base. All men are afraid in battle. The coward is the one who lets his fear overcome his sense of duty. Duty is the essence of manhood."
~General George S. Patton

"The most intense patriotism always flourishes in the rear."
~Aleksandr Solzhenitsyn, Nobel Prize in Literature in 1970

"Courage, above all things, is the first quality of a warrior."
~Carl von Clausewitz

RESOLUTENESS is a form of courage based on inner conviction or a deep commitment to a moral principle that results in tenaciously fighting for or enduring for that belief.[13]

"Lead me, follow me or get out of my way."
~General George S. Patton

"Be courageous. I have seen many depressions in business. Always America has emerged from these stronger and more prosperous. Be brave as your fathers before you. Have faith! Go forward!"
~Thomas A. Edison

CHIVALRY as courage takes on the qualities of knightly virtues. We might add heroism, gallantry, courtesy and graciousness toward the weak and helpless, reminiscent of medieval knighthood. And here Jon Johnson makes the case that Jesus Christ embodied the best of knightly virtues. He says that Jesus

"journeyed forth, clad in armor of a peerless manhood, to shield the defenseless, promote the holy and reveal a sacrificial life that would inspire the world. He stands forever as the Knight of knights... Jesus reached out to the sick and dying, pitied the possessed, comforted the mentally ill, raised the dead."[14]

And for his service, the Great Physician was first asked to leave the region and was ultimately crucified when he would not forsake the mission.

Jesus followed an inner agenda of love, and it took great courage to do it in his day and time. He socialized with the Samaritans, healed them and pointed them to God; he even made one of them a star of a parable. He was accused, *"You* are a Samaritan!" as if this were the most derogatory thing they could say. One of the most chivalrous and courageous things you and I can do is to confront entrenched prejudice.

In spite of being made a target of abuse, Jesus unflinchingly pursued his course, obeying his mandates to be the Son of God and to show us how to follow the path of personal Christhood.

Jesus boldly defended the women of his day. In those times, adulterous men could be ignored, but not so with women. When one adulterous woman was caught and brought to him, Jesus had to decide whether to stand on Mosaic Law, which said she should be stoned, or courageously point out to her accusers the need for some self-examination. The result was the extension of forgiveness toward one and some pointed self-examination for others regarding their own guilt and anger. These are actions of courage that demonstrated chivalry, fortitude and resoluteness.

Perhaps the greatest act of chivalry is offering to die for others. "Greater love has no one than this, that one lay down his life for his friends,"[15] the Bible tells us. Jesus compassionately chose to give his life in order to show the way, the truth and the life for all. And many others, unknown to us, have done the same.

Courage is not always "heroic" but it almost always involves some sort of action—the kind of action that sets you apart from the crowd or makes you independent of the crowd's approval. This kind of action is usually in harmony with your inner self that you have co-created with God. It's a kind of inner boldness that is based on your convictions rather than expediency or going along to get along. Most of the time these kinds of actions are not perceived as heroic, but they are courageous.

If you are courageous, you'll constantly be involved in similar but far less dramatic actions like returning lost money, telling it straight to an addicted friend, voting your conscience, confessing directly to another that you have wronged them in your thoughts with criticism, standing up for someone who is being bullied by others, or writing a letter to the editor of your local paper and revealing your name and address.

Courage does *not* mean impulsively or constantly avenging every wrong or correcting every inaccuracy. Often the most courageous action is to patiently wait for the right time and opportunity.

"Courage is what it takes to stand up and speak; courage is also what it takes to sit down and listen."
~Winston Churchill

Sometimes courage is endurance, constancy, commitment and faithfulness—staying in the game despite the slings and arrows of criticism and condemnation and having everyone point out to you how unsuccessful you are in your efforts.

Spend a few minutes watching a toddler who is learning to walk. That's courage in action. You don't fall up a mountain. You reach the summit by taking one step after another.

"If you have the courage to begin, you have the courage to succeed."
~David Viscott

"Life shrinks or expands in proportion to one's courage."
~Anais Nin

"Being deeply loved by someone gives you strength, while loving someone deeply gives you courage."
~Lao Tzu

In the foreword of Jon Johnson's book *Courage*, Senator Mark Hatfield of Oregon describes a time when he visited Mother Teresa in Calcutta, India. He traveled around the city with her, observing the total poverty, despair, filth and disease. And he asked her how she could keep on doing this when it seemed to make no real difference—there was no chance of overcoming the enormous need.[16] She replied:

> *"God did not ask me to be successful; he only asked me to be faithful."*
> ~Mother Teresa

This is the power of a personal example of courage for the entire world to see. Mother Teresa's example can be an essential guidepost for each one of us. Are you reluctant to move forward with courage in some cases because you are *afraid* you will not be successful? Success may not be the only goal when your inner guidance knows action is called for. Then you summon your courage, which in this case may look like a committed resoluteness. Mother Teresa's example can help all of us be more alert to those cases where there has been success only because there has been complete courage.

> *"Unless you have courage, a courage that keeps you going, always going, no matter what happens, there is no certainty of success. It is really an endurance race."*
> ~Henry Ford, *The Theosophist*, February, 1930

CHAPTER 5:
Having Courage

*"True strength is keeping everything together when everyone
expects you to fall apart."*
~Unknown

As a young woman in my early married life, we lived and worked
at a naval air station in California. Many of our friends were young
men who served in various branches of our Armed Forces. They
were active military personnel who came to study and be trained in
weaponry. In off hours, I heard them share Viet Nam war era stories
of incredibly courageous and fearful moments and episodes.

One story told by the comrades of a young pilot spoke of his
aircraft being shot up, and his miraculously making it back to the
aircraft carrier knowing he could not land on the carrier deck until
all other aircraft were safely recovered. So he had to circle around
until all other aircraft had landed and the ship's crew was able to
set up a giant net to catch his plane so he could crash-land on the
small and rolling surface of the aircraft carrier. This was the first
such attempt in the history of Navy avionics, and it was successful.
Certainly it required courage.

*"Courage is not living without fear. Courage is being scared to
death and doing the right thing anyway."*
~Chae Richardson

Another pilot was shot down over the jungle. He had to eject
from the aircraft only 200 yards above ground and landed on an ant
hill. He had to will his body not to move a muscle because there
were Viet Cong all around who would kill him or take him prisoner
if they discovered him before rescue helicopters could locate him

and get him out alive. Again, this required courage and a strong will to command his emotions and his body to remain still no matter what else was happening.

> *"I learned that courage was not the absence of fear, but the triumph over it. The brave man is not he who does not feel afraid, but he who conquers that fear."*
> ~Nelson Mandela

Perhaps this kind of courage is best acknowledged by Stephen Covey, who said:

> *"Courage is not the absence of fear, but the awareness that something else is more important."*
> ~Stephen Covey

CHAPTER 6:
Practicing Courage

"Confidence and courage comes through preparation and practice."
~Anonymous

The courage in some of the stories in the previous chapter is probably a form of courage based on a sense of desperation. What were their choices? What else could they do?

Where does such courage come from? Sometimes we have the opportunity to practice what might require extreme courage. One young warrior I spoke with was very tall, 6'4", and I asked about his experiences in survival training to become a Navy pilot. He shared that they had to practice some elements of physical and mental torture and deprivation so they would have experience in *enduring* if they were captured.

He was placed in a small box where he could not lie down, stand up or even stand hunched over. He could only squat or sit with his legs scrunched up. He endured it for many hours knowing they would let him out as soon as he "gave up" whatever they were requiring of him. I asked him if he was ever ready to give up and he said, "All the time." He shared with me that the only way he could keep going was to tell himself that he would endure it just another two to three minutes and then he would give up. Then another two to three minutes... and then another.

"Courage is fear that has said its prayers."
~Karle Wilson Baker, *Dreamers on Horseback*

In 1972, an airplane crash-landed high on a glacier in the Andes Mountains. I read the account given by Nando Parrado,[17] one of the members of a rugby team who survived the seventy-two-day ordeal. Without food or hope of rescue, he and one other traveler walked more than eighty miles out for help but not until all of them had already experienced nearly two-and-a-half months of trying to eat shoes and even suitcases, and were finally forced to nourish themselves from their dead companions. He said it was so cold they could feel their blood thicken and their tears were ice. When the cold became unbearable they would encourage one another with the simplest of goals: "Breathe one more time," they would say. "If you can breathe, you are not dead. Just breathe one more time."

"Either life entails courage, or it ceases to be life."
~E. M. Forster, *Paros and Pharillan*

How many times have you breathed since you began reading this book? How many times will you breathe in the next two-and-a-half months? What if all of those breaths were under the extremes just described?

"Courage is fear holding on a minute longer."
~General George S. Patton

Sometimes we see on the TV news a story of someone who has performed some kind of heroic rescue of someone else—like jumping into a river and saving someone or rescuing an animal. And the reporter will call them a hero. Usually they reply, "No. I just did what any responsible person would have done if they had been there."

That's what these young military men who shared their stories said. "It was my job." In other words, it was the path they were on and they summoned what was needed to live through it and complete the job.

Individuals or teams who train and pursue strengthening or perfecting the physical body often experience coming up against a performance wall that they don't seem to be able to break through. Others experience painful injuries that reduce their ability to perform as they did previously. When these individuals make the choice to be determined to pursue the healing, the nutrition or the training necessary to reach specific performance ratings, they are practicing courage. No doubt the rugby team whose story we just shared had practice in teamwork, in encouraging one another, in pushing through tough times together.

We can all practice courage in more ordinary ways, too. It does take courage to demonstrate the kind of determination and discipline to persevere through pain, disappointment or the discouragement of others in our lives. This need for determination or discipline in striving shows up for all of us in different ways. And so there are more ways to both practice and develop courage.

CHAPTER 7:
Developing Courage

"I wanted you to see what real courage is, instead of getting the idea that courage is a man with a gun in his hand. It's when you know you're licked before you begin, but you begin anyway and see it through no matter what."
~Atticus Finch, in Harper Lee's *To Kill a Mockingbird*

Now that we have looked at several forms of courage, can you call yourself a courageous person, at least in some things? I would say that everyone has the virtue of courage within them, though sometimes you choose a path or course of action with timidity because you don't yet know what kind of courage it will take.

So how do you develop courage as a virtue? How do you practice it—make it a habit—make it a part of your calling? I'm sure there are many creative ways that might work for you. I offer these three as a starting point:

1. CHOOSE A TEACHER. One way is to select a teacher—a model—just as author Jon Johnson illustrated through the word and works of Jesus Christ. Can you think of others whom you believe have demonstrated courage or are demonstrating it now in the present? Select one or more individuals and study their ways, their habits, their actions, their character and what they said or wrote—their quotations. This is one of the great things about books of quotations! Practice those elements that might work for you.

"Look around you—there are people around you. Maybe you will remember one of them all your life and later eat your heart out because you didn't make use of the opportunity to ask him questions. And the less you talk, the more you'll hear."
~Aleksandr Solzhenitsyn, *The Gulag Archipelago*

2. BUILD COMMUNITY. Taking actions with a partner or within a group of people means finding ways together to support, sponsor, foster and inspire one another with courage or hope. Most of us need community and can't make it without some form of community. A prime example is the proliferation of gangs in the face of family disintegration, lack of economic opportunity and the void of spiritual education.

Some of us might leave off striving for courage or any other virtue because we don't really see anyone else as a teacher, an example, or a model, or we do not have anyone to give us a sense of community to encourage us on the way. And in that word—*encourage*—we discover a prime *role for community* as well as a way to practice developing courage.

Every day we see individuals in the news or in our own families, schools, and workplaces who are practicing courage. They are striving. For many of them it seems as if no one is watching. No one saw them fall down or experience a crushing or humiliating defeat of some kind. No one seems to care, so why bother striving and pushing through hardships and setbacks to a victory waiting to be revealed?

Developing and practicing courage means paying attention! It means noticing what is going on with others—and then making the opportunity to *encourage* them. Just like the people who are striving to heal, overcome injuries or get past the next hurdle, most of us have a need for coaches or trainers to observe and assist us.

One way to be a responsible member of your community and to both develop and practice your courage is to be a kind of coach—the kind of coach who looks for opportunities to *encourage others*.

3. PRACTICE GRATITUDE. Practicing gratitude is an essential element in developing the virtue of courage. It's pretty easy to thank others for gifts, for acts of kindness or support they have provided to you. And you definitely should develop the habit of reinforcing others when they offer such gifts or the gift of themselves to you in walking through life.

One of the most important elements in practicing gratitude is to begin by being grateful for what *is*—just the way it *is*. This may not be the easiest form of gratitude to develop. Whether you consider the current conditions of your life to be good or bad, the circumstances of your present life can be your greatest teachers.

CHAPTER 8:
What Is Past Is Prologue

It is important to consider that what we *think* about the current conditions of our lives is very powerful because whether we think they are good or bad, we are creating our own reality. We all learn from the past, and truthfully, we can learn as much from a bad example as we can from a good one. That's what I mean when I say that the past and current conditions of our lives are our greatest teachers.

"What is past is prologue" is inscribed on statuary titled *Future* (1935, Robert Aiken) at the National Archives Building in Washington, D.C. It is also a line quoted from Shakespeare's play *The Tempest*. In general, a prologue points to the influence of history and sets the stage for what is yet to come in the future.

There are many quotes by numerous authors based on the theme that those who don't know or understand history are doomed to repeat it. Some people call this *karma*. Karma is our greatest teacher. While karma is an important part of many religions, it is also a very practical term when talking about the law of cause and effect in our lives. For every effect there is a cause.

> *"Luck is a word devoid of sense.*
> *Nothing can exist without a cause."*
> ~Voltaire

Spiritual teacher and author Elizabeth Clare Prophet wrote:

> *"We've all grown up learning about karma. We just didn't call*
> *it that. Instead we heard: What goes around comes around.*
> *Whatsoever a man soweth that shall he also reap. For every action*

> *there is an equal and opposite reaction...In essence, karma tells*
> *us that whatever we do will come full circle to our doorstep—*
> *sometime, somewhere."*[18]
> *"Your believing or not believing in karma has no effect on its*
> *existence, nor on its consequences to you. Just as a refusal to*
> *believe in the ocean would not prevent you from drowning."*
> ~F. Paul Wilson, *The Tomb*

In Sanskrit, the word *karma* means act, action, word or deed. Elizabeth Clare Prophet tells us:

> *"The law of karma as it is traditionally taught says that our*
> *thoughts, words and deeds—positive and negative—create a*
> *chain of cause and effect, and that we will personally experience*
> *the effect of every cause we have set in motion. Karma, therefore,*
> *is our greatest benefactor, returning to us the good we have sent to*
> *others. It is also our greatest teacher, allowing us to learn from our*
> *mistakes...The law of karma is the law of love. There is no greater*
> *love than having the opportunity to understand the consequences*
> *of our action—or our inaction—so that our soul can grow."*[19]

Aleksandr Solzhenitsyn, a Russian novelist, historian, and short story writer, was an outspoken critic of the Soviet Union and was only allowed to publish one work in the Soviet Union. Subsequently, he published mostly in the West, and was awarded the 1970 Nobel Prize in Literature. In 1973 he published *The Gulag Archipelago* and was expelled from the Soviet Union in 1974, but returned to Russia in 1994 after the dissolution of the Soviet Union. He wrote:

> *"It was granted me to carry away from my prison years on my*
> *bent back, which nearly broke beneath its load, this essential*
> *experience; how a human being becomes evil and how good. In*
> *the intoxication of youthful successes I had felt myself to be*
> *infallible, and I was therefore cruel. In the surfeit of power I*
> *was a murderer, and an oppressor. In my most evil moments I*
> *was convinced that I was doing good, and I was well supplied*

with systematic arguments. And it was only when I lay there on rotting prison straw that I sensed within myself the first stirrings of good. Gradually it was disclosed to me that the line separating good and evil passes not through states, nor between classes, nor between political parties either—but right through every human heart—and through all human hearts. This line shifts. Inside us it oscillates with the years. And even within hearts overwhelmed by evil, one small bridgehead of good is retained. And even in the best of all hearts, there remains. . . an unuprooted small corner of evil."
~Aleksandr Solzhenitsyn

"Is there one maxim which ought to be acted upon throughout one's whole life? Surely it is the maxim of loving-kindness: Do not unto others what you would not have them do unto you."
~Confucius

To take on the wisdom Confucius shares requires great courage. It takes maturity of the heart and a proper exercise of our free will. Karma is directly related to free will and shows how we hold the keys to our destiny.

"Courage is the virtue of the free."
~Daniel Quinn, *The Holy*

"Be grateful even for hardship, setbacks, and bad people. Dealing with such obstacles is an essential part of training in the Art of Peace."
~Morihei Ueshiba

"The law of karma. . .is not intended to act as a lash, to tear apart the souls of men. The law of karma is intended to instruct and to cause mankind to approach the throne of grace without fear, with the clearness of mind and being that will render them able to receive the pure vibratory action of Almighty God."
~Annice Booth, *The Path to Your Ascension*

"The holistic doctrine of Karma gives us a reason for everything and everything for a reason. Karma, as a philosophy, maintains hope in the midst of hopelessness and provides us with the courage to continue our personal evolution."
~Jonn Mumford, *Karma Manual*

"Karma is the record of services. Karma is the term used in Buddhist teaching. Taoists use the term 'te.' Christians use the term 'deed.' Many other spiritual beings use the term 'virtue.' Karma, te, deed, and virtue are the same thing but in different words. To understand karma is to understand all of these words."
~Zhi Gang Sha, *The Power of Soul*

Developing courage requires being grateful for what *is* and then learning from it and taking the next actions.

CHAPTER 9:
Courage Is a Path to Freedom

"No negative state, no compromising or otherwise self-defeating thought or feeling, is your 'original equipment.'"
~Guy Finley, *The Courage to Be Free*

Courage as a virtue or character trait has proven to be inextricably linked to *truth*—truth as we are given to know it in the moment we are required to act. "The truth shall set you free" is a quotation many of us are familiar with. As recorded in the Bible in John 8:32, Jesus said this to his disciples. It is also used in academic circles to promote academic freedom and the power of learning.

What about the kind of courage we need in order to perceive the truth about ourselves? Courage doesn't always show up only on the outside for all to see. The kind of courage that is needed to stand, face and conquer our unseen and unheard thoughts, feelings, emotions and criticisms of ourselves and others is also necessary in order to be free.

Guy Finley, spiritual teacher, author and speaker,[20] in his book *The Courage to Be Free: Discover Your Original Fearless Self*, offers profound insight as he encourages us to act on what we know is true.[21] Finley outlines principles of courage that can assist us in reclaiming our right to be free. And these principles don't require the cooperation or permission of anyone else. Practicing these principles lies totally within the level of command you choose to take in your own life. To know this one thing can produce freedom you may never have known before.

Finley says the reason we tend to "lose the command we long for" is due to "a certain kind of spiritual forgetfulness."[22]

"In our moment of need, we can't remember the part of us that can't
be made to serve anything not of its own choosing."
~Guy Finley

When we decide to remember the truth that we can put our negative thoughts and feelings "in their proper place," we can regain self-command, and with it, more peace of mind and freedom. Finley wrote:

"Remember that all dark thoughts and feelings require our consent
to punish us and that these negative states are, in themselves,
literally nothing without the powers we grant them. Then, in this
same bright moment of recalling the truth of ourselves we are made
the conqueror of what would overcome us!"[23]

"We must remember that there is no intelligence in any worry,
anger, or fear, and then have the courage to act on
our understanding."[24]

"Pain is neither a natural nor necessary part of
making a mistake."[25]

"Reliving the past is powerless to change a present
misunderstanding."[26]

Finley expands on these principles saying:

"Beating ourselves up after making a blunder doesn't mean that we
actually knew better than what we just did—nor does this kind of
suffering lead to greater command or better decisions the next time
around. Self-punishing acts prove only one thing: Something in us
would rather suffer over what happened in the past than be present
to those parts of us that erred in the first place. Real self-command
dawns within us as we realize that reliving the past is powerless to
change a present understanding; it comes from the light of our new
knowledge that having the courage to drop the level of Self that
keeps wronging us and others is far more important than being seen
as right. This same realization also grants us the courage to start
life over—again and again."[27]

"We should always remember one thing whenever the inner-going gets tough, which it must if we are to grow. It is far better for us to temporarily fail at becoming what we intend to be, than it is to succeed at remaining who and what we have been."
~Guy Finley, *Let Go and Live in the Now*[28]

"It is not the critic who counts; not the man who points out how the strong man stumbles, or where the doer of deeds could have done them better. The credit belongs to the man who is actually in the arena, whose face is marred by dust and sweat and blood; who strives valiantly; who errs, who comes short again and again, because there is no effort without error and shortcoming; but who does actually strive to do the deeds; who knows great enthusiasms, the great devotions; who spends himself in a worthy cause; who at the best knows in the end the triumph of high achievement, and who at the worst, if he fails, at least fails while daring greatly, so that his place shall never be with those cold and timid souls who neither know victory nor defeat.."
~President Theodore Roosevelt[29]
(Excerpt from the speech "Citizenship in a Republic," 1910)

CHAPTER 10:
Courage Is the Coming of Age of the Heart

*"The greatest test of courage on the earth is to bear defeat
without losing heart."*
~R. G. Ingersoll

Courage is not for the faint of heart. So it can be wise to practice courage. For some, thanking God and praising Him for everything, including our so-called sufferings, is one good way to practice courage. It's easy to observe how we complain because of this or that, some little inconvenience in our life or service, something that doesn't work right—the car breaks down and we get inharmonious and complain. You and I can instead reverse the energy and praise and thank God for testing our soul, immediately, right then and there, when it happens! This is an example of practicing gratitude for what *is*.

This practice also develops maturity of the heart. The root word of courage comes from the Old French *corage*, in turn from the Latin *cor*, meaning *heart*. And courage is a habit of *gratitude of the heart*. Practicing gratitude is a chance, an opportunity, to practice courage through a continuous sense or awareness of holding gratefulness within your heart.

It is through this practice that all of us are tried and strengthened. Spirit can and will strengthen you so that you are not left in a state in which everything is done for you and everything works out perfectly—this would make you flabby. You wouldn't have any drive or "muscle" to figure out solutions to life. You are given difficult situations so you can practice courage and be strengthened.

"Great spirits have always found violent opposition from mediocrities. The latter cannot understand it when a man does not thoughtlessly submit to hereditary prejudices but honestly and courageously uses his intelligence."
~Albert Einstein

"To go against the dominant thinking of your friends, of most of the people you see every day, is perhaps the most difficult act of heroism you can have."
~Theodore H. White

"One can never consent to creep when one feels an impulse to soar."
~Helen Keller

"The simple step of a courageous individual is not to take part in the lie... One word of truth outweighs the world."
~Aleksandr Solzhenitsyn

"For, in the final analysis, our most common link is that we all inhabit this small planet. We all breathe the same air. We all cherish our children's future. And we are all mortal."
~John F. Kennedy, *Profiles in Courage*

Courage doesn't always roar. Sometimes courage is the quiet voice at the end of the day saying, 'I will try again tomorrow.'"
~Mary Anne Radmacher

I will try again tomorrow. This is indeed the kind of courage to grow for daily living. It is a demonstration of maturity that points to the coming of age of your heart.

"Let your light shine.
Be a source of strength and courage.
Share your wisdom.
Radiate love."
~Wilferd Peterson

ENDNOTES

1 Lady Master Venus, *Pearls of Wisdom*, Vol. 36 No. 8, www.tsl.org

2 Alberta Fredricksen, *Transforming Everyday Conflict: Tools, Tips and Roadmaps to Better Communication and Stronger Relationships*, HeartPeace Now Publications, www.HeartPeaceNow.com

3 Saint Germain, "The Crucible of Being," in *Saint Germain On Alchemy*, p. 99

4 John F. Kennedy, *Profiles in Courage*, http://www.jfklibrary.org

5 Ibid.

6 Ibid.

7 Ibid.

8 Jon Johnson, *Courage: You Can Stand Strong in the Face of Fear*, Copyright 1990 by SP Publications, Victor Books, Wheaton, IL 60187

9 Ibid.

10 Ibid., p. 35

11 Ibid., p. 36

12 Ibid., pp. 38-39

13 Ibid., pp. 39-40

14 Ibid., pp. 36-37

15 John 15:13

16 Jon Johnson, *Courage: You Can Stand Strong in the Face of Fear*, p. 7

17 Nando Parrado, *Miracle in the Andes*, with Vince Rause, Three Rivers Press, www.crownpublishing.com

18 Elizabeth Clare Prophet with Patricia R. Spadaro, *Karma and Reincarnation*, p. 2, Copyright © Summit University Press, www.tsl.org

[19] Ibid.

[20] Guy Finley, www.guyfinley.com and www.guyfinley.org/about/life-of-learning

[21] Guy Finley, *The Courage to Be Free: Discover Your Original Fearless Self*, Red Wheel/Weiser, LLC, Copyright © 2010 by Guy Finley, www.redwheelweiser.com

[22] Ibid., p. 48

[23] Guy Finley, *Let Go and Live in the Now: Awaken the Peace, Power, and Happiness in Your Heart*, Red Wheel/Weiser, LLC, Copyright © 2004 Guy Finley, www.redwheel/weiser.com. p. 175

[24] Guy Finley, *The Courage to Be Free: Discover Your Original Fearless Self*, Red Wheel/Weiser, LLC, Copyright © 2010 by Guy Finley, www.redwheelweiser.com. p. 52

[25] Ibid., p. 54

[26] Ibid., p. 55

[27] Ibid.

[28] Guy Finley, *Let Go and Live in the Now: Awaken the Peace, Power, and Happiness in Your Heart*, Red Wheel/Weiser, LLC, Copyright © 2004 Guy Finley, www.redwheel/weiser.com

[29] Ibid., quoted in *Let Go and Live in the Now*, p. 185

ABOUT THE AUTHOR

Alberta V. Fredricksen
Founder of HeartPeace Now
Coach, Trainer, Author
www.HeartPeaceNow.com

Alberta is passionate about helping others. Her life's work combines many years of professional experience and a spirituality that honors and looks beyond the outer crust into the precious spirit within every person. Through the wisdom Alberta has garnered, she deftly guides clients to use the presence of existing conflict as a platform to gain a personal mastery of effective communication skills and to achieve fulfilling relationships.

Alberta's training and experiences as a human resource administrator, educator, public school site administrator, negotiator for labor and management, coach, trainer, consultant, minister and mediator have refined her conflict and life coaching expertise in both cooperative and adversarial circumstances representing and teaching diverse individuals and groups.

A natural coach and teacher, Alberta's expertise, specialized training and life experiences provide a wide repertoire of choices, tools, strategies, formulas and stories to illustrate for her clients the process of resolving expectations and to help them gain a personal mastery in managing and transforming everyday conflict.

A Special FREE Gift for Readers of GROWING COURAGE: Self-Empowerment for Facing Life's Challenges—Quotes, Stories & Insights

Alberta wants you to receive *"What Does It Mean to Be Confident?"*

In a special concise PDF companion report you'll learn more about:

- Being capable
- Owning your own thoughts and feelings
- Endurance
- Self-nurturance

And you can participate in a self-directed activity for discovering more about your personal values.

Don't miss this opportunity to learn more about growing relationships and moving through life with greater confidence.

Visit *www.HeartPeaceNow.com/confident* to request your free copy today!

Thank you for reading my book! I hope that you found it to be inspiring and helpful in some personal way for your life.

In our busy world, filled with options and distractions, book reviews mean even more than they did in the past. If you enjoyed my book, I'd be grateful and honored for you to leave a review on www.Amazon.com.

Just enter the title: *Growing Courage* or my name as author, Alberta V. Fredricksen.

May your life be blessed with HeartPeace Now!
Alberta